LEFT FOOT FIRST: A FAITHFUL MIRACLE TO FINANCIAL ASTROLOGY

ACHARYA AMITESH KUMAR DWIVEDI

To all my readers

Contents

Foreword

What is science? What is miracle? There is very very little difference that sometimes it is very difficult to recognise. This book brings forth some practice and rituals that are well practiced by the author himself and that bore result. Yes result! Because without result everything is just zero, just great zero. So, practice this faithfully and get the benefits of this ancient knowledge applied to modern Era and live happily and win.

Yes, it is the miraculous secrets of left foot.

Preface

Simple techniques to live and prosper happily. Only one has to adhere to rules and have faith on almighty and not to offend anyone.

Acknowledgements

To the ancient sages who discovreed it.

Prologue

What is science? What is miracle? There is very very little difference that sometimes it is very difficult to recognise. This book brings forth some practice and rituals that are well practiced by the author himself and that bore result. Yes result! Because without result everything is just zero, just great zero. So, practice this faithfully and get the benefits of this ancient knowledge applied to modern Era and live happily and win.

Yes, it is the miraculous secrets of left foot.

CHAPTER ONE

Which man has a lot of money? Learn about the symptoms of rich people There are several signs of the body that are always present in rich people. According to the plamistry, rich people will be forced to have all these marks on their bodies. Plamistry is an important subject of Hindu scriptures. This is mainly due to the structure of the limbs and more than a few signs of the body can give a clear idea about the personality and future of men and women. Today we will discuss which body signs will tell you that you are a rich person. There are several signs of the body that are always present in rich people. According to the plamistry, rich people will be forced to have all these marks on their bodies. Basically the line of the hand, the sesame of the hand, the line of destiny, the mark of the palm of the hand, the shape of the thumb - all this makes it very clear how much money will come into the hands of that person. According to the marine scriptures, if the rich have these marks in their hands, they can spend their whole lives happily. Take a look at the signs- 1. Palm The palm of the hand must be deep. It is considered very auspicious to have a small sesame in the palm of the hand. If there is a bow mark in the hand then it is also auspicious. If there is a yes mark on the thumb then it is good. According to the plamistry, if these signs exist, this person will never run out of money. Thumb- The barley mark on the thumb is auspicious. Money is considered a sign of arrival. This sign is of knowledge and meaning. Even if the finger is long, it paves the way for money. 3. Sesame- According to palmistry, a person becomes rich if he has temple symbol, flag, Capricorn symbol in his hand. On the other hand, if a man has a black sesame in the middle of his hand, it is very auspicious. That person will get a lot of respect as well as money. Arrow marks in hand- Those who have bow marks in their hands are meaningful. Sword in hand, spear mark is considered auspicious. These signs make money. If there is such a sign, the person concerned can hold a high position in administrative bodies like army and police.

CHAPTER TWO

This special line is in the hands of one in a thousand people, which brings a lot of resources The line of the hand tells how a person will live. Such as his financial status, career, married life, fame, family, health, etc. Will he get the full result of his hard work or not? Calculations are made based on the position of the line, the statistics, the marks on the palm, the nature of the person, the behavior and the future. The line of the hand tells how a person will live. Such as his financial status, career, married life, fame, family, health, etc. Will he get the full result of his hard work or not? The special condition of these lines shines Some lines are considered very important in handicrafts.

These lines are - heart line, life line, marriage line and destiny line. By looking at the position of these lines, it is clear whether they will give good results or bad results. First of all, not everyone has these lines in their hands, and those who have them in their hands, as well as in a happy position, rarely do so. Today we will talk about the line of destiny which is in the hands of very few people. Besides, every day of the life of those who have a happy position in their hands is happy. Destiny shines like a line of destiny The line that comes from the lower part of the palm to Saturn under the middle finger is called the line of destiny. If the line starts from the bracelet and goes straight to the Saturn mountain or meets the base of the middle finger, it is considered very auspicious. If this line is not torn and deep, the person will not only get a lot of wealth, but also high position and a lot of respect in his life. Wherever such people go, they create their own identity. If the line of destiny starts from the region of the moon and goes to the mountain of Saturn, then that person gets success in everything. Such people get a lot of respect in their life and also give respect to every human being. So such people are very popular among the people. On the other hand, those whose destiny line starts from the life line and goes to the Saturn mountain, never run out of money in their life. These people always have a lot of money and they live a very prosperous life.

CHAPTER THREE

According to Acharya Chanakya, there are five ways to become a millionaire, try it yourself According to Chanakya, a person who wants to be a millionaire in his life must pay attention to some important things. Today we will tell you some things related to Chanakya principle, which if followed will always have the grace of mother Lakshmi on you Acharya Chanakya is considered to be the first great economist and philosopher not only in India but also in the world. Apart from economics, politics, diplomacy, Acharya Chanakya said a lot about practical life, which is as useful for today's society as ever. Chanakya says in his policy that a person's success and failure depends on his habits. Mother Lakshmi's blessings are always on those who have good habits. There is no lack of resources and facilities for that person. According to Chanakya, a person who wants to be a millionaire in his life must pay attention to some important things. Today we will tell you something related to the Chanakya principle, which if followed will always have the grace of Mother Lakshmi on you and will continue to rain money on you. Chanakya has given some lessons to the elders, the elderly and the children in his policy. By following which man can make his life successful. Today we will tell you the secret of Chanakya, by following which you too can fill your house with happiness and prosperity. You have to work hard According to Chanakya, Mother Lakshmi is always pleased with the person who works diligently and sincerely and blesses that person. Such people never run out of money. And he is always moving forward. He believed that hard work was the key to becoming a millionaire. Proceed as planned The first step to success in any endeavor is to come up with a complete plan. Always create a strategy before starting any work, then you will never fail. And since the work is successful, mother Lakshmi is pleased with such people. Follow an orderly lifestyle According to Chanakya, if you want to achieve success and respect in your life, then you should follow an orderly lifestyle. According to him, the person who succeeds in his life is the one who completes every task with discipline and gives importance to time. Take on the challenge with courage Chanakya mentioned that in order to be successful, one has to face all kinds of challenges. The person who is never afraid to take on challenges is always successful in his life. Donate some of the earnings According to Chanakya, the person who moves forward in life with everyone and distributes profits properly to every person, becomes very rich. According to Chanakya, a person who donates a portion of his earnings to the poor and does good to mankind, the blessings of Mother Lakshmi are always upon him. Also, do not use your money to harm anyone.

CHAPTER FOUR

crystal tree

Keep crystal trees at home or in the office, you will get the fruits in a few days There are many sayings in feng shui based on the Panchatattva, which, if kept at home, in the office or in the garden, destroy the negative energy around the person. And there are good results in life. Today we are going to tell you some rules related to crystal tree etc., which if followed will bring happiness and prosperity in the house. Like Indian ecology, feng shui is Chinese ecology. Feng Shui also works to promote positive energy. There are many sayings in feng shui that maintain happiness and prosperity in the home. There are many sayings in feng shui based on the Panchatattva, which, if kept at home, in the office or in the garden, destroy the negative energy around the person. And there are good results in life. Today we are going to tell you some rules related to crystal tree etc., which if followed will bring happiness and prosperity in the house. How about a crystal tree? Regularly keeping the crystal tree mentioned in feng shui at home or in the office can bring a lot of changes in one's life. The crystal tree is made of different colored gems and glass. You can keep this crystal tree at home or in the office of your choice. The benefits of planting crystal trees at home or in the office-Many benefits of crystal tree have been mentioned in feng shui. It is recommended to plant a crystal tree to awaken the good fortune of the house or to maintain strength in married life. It is considered auspicious to place a crystal tree on the southwest side of the living room or bedroom. According to feng shui scriptures, placing a crystal tree on the northwest side of the house solves the financial problems of the house. Not only that, there are career and business opportunities. According to feng shui, the eastern part of the house is related to health. So if you put a crystal tree on the east side of the house or office, the health of the people is good. To progress in studies, a person is advised to keep a crystal tree in the shape of his study. Positive results are obtained by placing the study at the waist or in the north-east corner of the study table. At the same time, keeping colorful crystal trees in the house maintains the energy balance in the house. Also the physical and mental problems of the person are eliminated.

CHAPTER FIVE

Never buy these five things on Saturday, it can be extremely miserable According to the scriptures, he is the god of justice. If he is at the top of the chart, the person will be successful in all tasks. And if Saturn is weak, various problems will occur. Saturday is the day of Lord Saturn. Worshiping Shani on this day brings good results and brings an end to bad days. Many beliefs about Saturday are also coming into our society. Some of these beliefs are psychological and some are related to astrology. According to the scriptures, he is the god of justice. If he is at the top of the chart, the person will be successful in all tasks. And if Saturn is weak, various problems will occur. How many totkars are mentioned in astrology. Which strengthens the space of Saturn. If Saturn's position is not strong then failure will not follow you. Even after a thousand attempts, success will not come for the position of Saturn. If the position of Saturn in the constellation is bad then there are various obstacles in life. Family complications continue from financial loss. With suffering. Unemployment, failing exams and even long-term physical complications can be the cause of Saturn's position. Find out what not to buy on Saturday ... Rot iron It is believed that Shanidev became angry when he bought iron items on Saturday. Things made of iron should be donated on this day. Donating iron purifies the wrath of Saturn and brings profit to the business of loss. Don't buy oil Avoid buying oil on this day. Although oil can be donated. Saturn's condition is eliminated by feeding black dog pudding made with mustard oil. According to astrology, buying mustard oil or any other substance on Saturday is beneficial. Don't buy shoes If you want to buy black shoes, don't buy on Saturday. It is believed that buying black shoes on Saturday brings failure to the wearer. Combustible substance Fuels, matches, kerosene, etc. are considered essential for cooking. In Indian culture, fire is considered a deity and special emphasis is placed on the purity of fuel but buying fuel on Saturdays is prohibited. It is said that the fuel brought home on Saturday brings problems to the family. Don't buy a broom The broom cleans the house of filth. This brings positive energy in the house. Saturdays are not considered suitable for buying brooms. Bringing a broom home on Saturday alleviates poverty.

CHAPTER SIX

Take the left foot first to subdue the anger, there are 5 easy ways in astrology, Anger is a psychological problem. Which is determined by our mood and the surrounding environment and the movement of the stars. For example, people in Scorpio, Leo and Taurus get into trouble because of their strong personality. Their anger is much more than others. Anger is the greatest enemy of any human being. Anger causes a lot of harm to many people. Again, there are some people who lose their temper even a little bit. And in that he brought the loss of his own life. Many people make wrong decisions because of anger. So it is very important to control anger. And there are five ways to do this in astrology. Anger is a psychological problem. Which is determined by our mood and the surrounding environment and the movement of the stars. For example, people in Scorpio, Leo and Taurus get into trouble because of their strong personality. Their anger is much more than others. Their personal and professional lives were damaged. However, they can control their anger through their environment and work environment. Let's take a look at five ways to control anger - which astrology agrees with. 1. Always keep your surroundings clean. Anger is thought to exist in people who are not clean around them. Light a lamp at home in the morning and in the evening. 2. In astrology, those who have anger problems should never insult women in the family and at work. They should worship Hanuman daily. Hanuman will benefit from reciting Challisa. 3. A vegetarian diet helps reduce anger. Avoid tamasic foods like onion, garlic. It is better not to eat spicy food and processed food. Absolutely do not eat chin. Quit alcohol, smoke intoxication. No drugs are good for them. 4. Get acquainted (gain, obtain) with present and future generations, and talk to relatives. Wake up and bow to Mother Earth. When you wake up, first put your left foot on the ground. Then remove the right leg. Remember not to talk to anyone for at least 15 minutes after getting out of bed. Doing this regularly will reduce anger. 5. It is important to wear a silver ring to control your anger. Because silver has the addition of moon. The moon is calm. Calms the mind. Those who get angry quickly get angry easily if they have a silver ring in their hand

CHAPTER SEVEN

Chanakya principle: If you stay away from these three habits, success will come in all the uses of life The Chanakya policy also addresses issues related to religion, money, women, occupation, friends and married life. The Chanakya principle gives a person an idea of how to behave in a situation. The Chanakya policy offers many important suggestions for making people's lives happier. It is said that a person who follows their principles will have many problems in his life. The Chanakya policy also addresses issues related to religion, money, women, occupation, friends and married life. The Chanakya principle gives a person an idea of how to behave in a situation. Chanakya says that if we want success in education and career, we should always stay away from bad habits. These habits only create obstacles. The key to success is to say that success in life lies in good qualities. That is, no goal is difficult for those who have good and noble qualities. They succeed. In the teachings of the Gita, Lord Krishna says that the person who adopts the best qualities is always happy. Such people get all kinds of happiness. Such a person also gets a lot of respect. Therefore, it is necessary to emphasize on adopting good qualities. Bad habits only hurt one person. Just as bad habits can harm you, so can bad habits. Bad habits are the biggest obstacle in education and career building. So these bad habits should be avoided. Laziness is man's greatest enemy According to scholars, a person who works hard should stay away from laziness. Laziness is an obstacle to success. Due to laziness, the individual is not able to take full advantage of the opportunity and the competitors go ahead. Such people have to suffer a lot later. Never waste time It is not a good habit to waste time. This is a bad habit. Time must be used properly. Time is very precious. One should understand the usefulness of time for education and career building and know the importance of time. Stay away from addiction According to scholars, intoxicants should not be taken. This is one of the worst habits. Bad habits attract more youth. So be careful. Addiction affects health as well as the mind and brain. This practice does the most damage to education and career. So you should not take any kind of drugs.